Hey Beauty!

Here's a list of things I want you to remember:

1. You have purpose.

2. You matter.

3. You have gifts to share with the world.

4. Your mind is brilliant.

5. You can do anything you put your mind to.

6. You are loved.

7. YOU ARE BEAUTIFUL INSIDE & OUT!

-TYIA

What Are Affirmations?

Affirmations are positive things you say about yourself!

This poem is an affirmation for you to say daily!

ISBN-13: 978-0-9986624-4-2
COPYRIGHT 2016 BY TYIA ADAIR
PUBLISHED BY A BEAUTIFUL, WONDERFUL ME

A Beautiful Wonderful Me
An Affirmation Activity Book

written by Tyia Lashe
photography by Ron Massey

this book belongs to:

_____

Dedication

This book is dedicated to the young queens who starred in this book!
You all are awesome! This book is also dedicated to the little girl I once
was. I pray that every little girl who reads this book is blessed & always
remembers that she is beautiful, wonderful, and one of a kind!

"...i am fearfully and wonderfully made..."
-Psalms 139:14

Hey Beauty!

Things you will need while reading:

-crayons
-tape
-creativity
-pictures of yourself

(if you don't have any pictures of yourself,
grab some paper and draw yourself!)

You will see why :)

I love how I look--
my hair, my skin, my eyes!
Every where I go,
my head stays held high!

I am a
beautiful, wonderful
me!

What 3 things do you love the most about yourself?

Write or draw them below!

TAPE A
PICTURE OF
YOU!

TAPE A
PICTURE OF
YOU!

My laugh is contagious!
My spirit shines bright!
Whenever there's darkness,
I always find the light!

I am a
beautiful, wonderful
me!

What are 3 things that make you happy?

Write or draw them below !

TAPE A
PICTURE
OF YOU LAUGHING!

TAPE A
PICTURE
OF YOU SMILING!

Love is what I spread!
Positivity is what I speak!
I strive to help others,
every day of the week!

I am a
beautiful, wonderful
me!

What are 3 ways that you can help someone or show love?

Write or draw them below!

TAPE A
PICTURE
OF YOU
BEING KIND!

TAPE A
PICTURE
OF YOU
HELPING SOMEONE!

Creativity flows out!
Never do I hold back!
My gifts will be shared,
I'll make sure of that!

I am a
beautiful, wonderful
me!

What gifts & talents do you have?

Write or draw them below!

TAPE A
PICTURE
OF YOU BEING
CREATIVE!

TAPE A
PICTURE OF
YOUR TALENT!

My mind is wide open!
I can learn anything!
I will tackle every problem
this life may bring!

I am a
beautiful, wonderful
me!

What are 3 things you want to learn how to do?

Write or draw them below!

TAPE A
PICTURE
OF YOU
LEARNING
SOMETHING
NEW!

TAPE A
PICTURE
OF YOU
LEARNING
SOMETHING
NEW!

I'm as bold as they come!
Doubt & fear are cast away!
I will follow my dreams!
Nothing will stand in my way!

I am a
beautiful, wonderful
me!

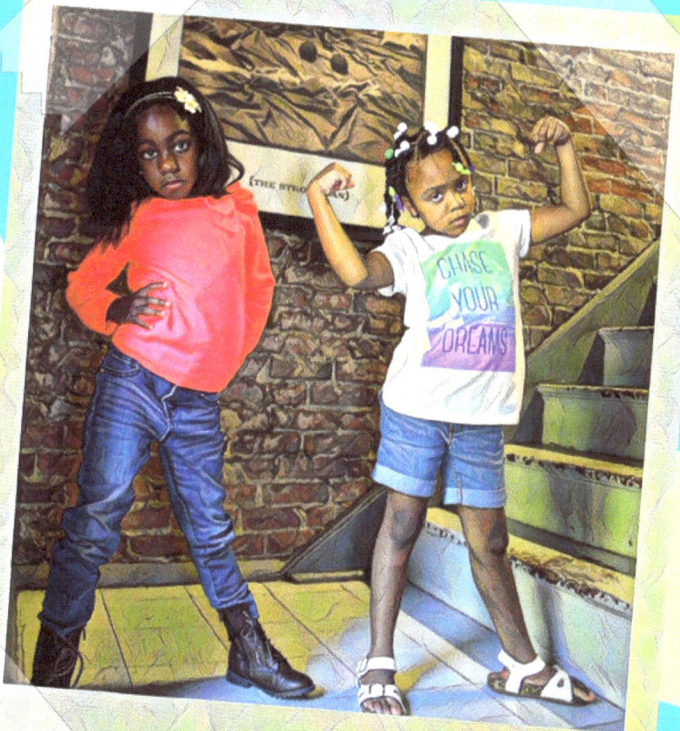

WHAT ARE YOUR DREAMS?

(EXAMPLE: BECOME A PAINTER, GET AN "A" ON A MATH TEST, CHANGE THE WORLD!)

Write or draw them below!

TAPE A
PICTURE
OF YOU
LIVING YOUR DREAM!

TAPE A
PICTURE
OF YOU
LIVING YOUR DREAM!

Every girl is different
in her own special way!
Embrace who you are!
Yell out and say. . .

I am a
beautiful, wonderful
me!

TAPE A
PICTURE OF
YOU IN YOUR
FAVORITE
OUTFIT!

TAPE A
PICTURE OF
YOU WEARING
YOUR FAVORITE
HAIRSTYLE!

affirmations to speak daily

1. I am worthy.

2. I am loved.

3. I have purpose.

4. I matter.

5. I have gifts.

6. I am beautiful.

7. I can do anything.

affirmations to speak daily

(create your own)

1.

2.

3.

4.

5.

6.

7.

About the Author

TYIA IS A SELF-PUBLISHED AUTHOR FROM KANSAS CITY, MO. SHE IS ON A MISSION TO USE HER WORDS TO EMPOWER YOUNG GIRLS TO BE THE BEST THEY CAN BE.

AS A CHILD, TYIA STRUGGLED WITH A NEGATIVE SELF-IMAGE. TYIA HID HER STRUGGLES BEHIND A SMILE AND IT HINDERED HER GREATLY. AS AN ADULT, TYIA FINALLY REALIZED THE POWER OF HAVING A POSITIVE SENSE OF SELF.

TYIA BELIEVES THAT WORDS HAVE POWER AND SHE WANTS TO INSPIRE GIRLS TO USE THEIR WORDS FOR GOOD!

Hi ! :)

STAY CONNECTED
Instagram: @tyialashe

Check out Tyia's other books for girls available on Amazon!

About ABWME

A BEAUTIFUL WONDERFUL ME

A BEAUTIFUL, WONDERFUL ME WAS CREATED TO EMPOWER GIRLS TO DISCOVER THE GREATNESS WITHIN THEMSELVES. ABWME IS ON A MISSION TO BUILD UP BOLD, FEARLESS, & COURAGEOUS YOUNG GIRLS BY PROMOTING SELF-LOVE, POSTIVITY, & CREATIVITY!

STAY CONNECTED:
WEBSITE: WWW.ABWME.COM

www.ingramcontent.com/pod-product-compliance
Lightning Source LLC
LaVergne TN
LVHW072056070426
835508LV00002B/132